WINDOWS

Things Made of Wood

HEINLE
CENGAGE Learning

Y|S|G
A YBM COMPANY

Young & Son
Global, Inc.

Contents

tree

wood

pencil

chair

paper towels

violin

1 tree

2

This is a tree.
Wood comes from trees.

③

paper

block

wood

bat

People use wood for many things.

pencil

A pencil is made of wood.
You write with a pencil.

book

A book is made from wood.
You read a book.

chair

A chair is made of wood.
You sit on a chair.

house

Some houses are made of wood.
You live in a house.

paper towels

Paper towels are made from wood. You clean with paper towels.

violin

A violin is made of wood.
Can you play the violin?

These things are made of wood. What are they?

Made of Wood

I live in a house that's made of wood,
Made of wood, made of wood.
I live in a house that's made of wood.
Wood comes from trees.

I read a book that's made from wood,
Made from wood, made from wood.
I read a book that's made from wood.
Wood comes from trees.

Index